The Splendid Little Book of
All Things Dog

by Bob Lovka

illustrations by Setsu Broderick

BOWTIE ™
P R E S S

To Leonard Stern, whose splendid sense of humor
makes him the "top dog" of comedy writing.
-B.L.
To Kyle, Raulie, Genna, and Parker
-S.B.

Ruth Berman, editor-in-chief
Nick Clemente, special consultant
Cathe Jacobi, designer

Library of Congress Cataloging-in-Publication Data

Lovka, Bob, Date.
    The splendid little book of all things dog / Bob Lovka ;
  illustrations by Setsu Broderick.
      p.   cm.
   ISBN 1-889540-27-7
   1. Dogs—Miscellanea. 2. Dogs—Health—Miscellanea.   I. Title.
   SF427.L7 1998
   636.7—dc21   97-32161
                                                          CIP

BowTie™ Press
3 Burroughs
Irvine, California 92618

Manufactured in the United States of America
First Printing April 1998
10 9 8 7 6 5 4 3 2

CONTENTS

A Note from Bob

Welcome to the rambunctious world of dogs!

This little book is about your best friend. Whether you elegantly stroll through town with your Afghan or borzoi, or romp in the backyard with your terrier or mutt, you'll find in this book supremely interesting facts, fun trivia, and helpful tips about living with your dog.

Some dogs might read this book by themselves—usually late at night when no one is watching—but most depend on you, the owner, master, big-dog-in-charge, to read it to them. Keeping in mind that Alsatians, shih tzus, and Samoyeds have a short attention span, the information has been kept, well, short.

Dealing with a dog brings all of life into play. There is frustration and exhilaration, laughter and despair. And vet bills. Yet, through it all there are those big eyes looking up at you and that tail wagging a mile a minute. No matter what the world does to you during the day, there's a bubbly, bounding welcome when you come home. Somebody is glad to see you. You matter.

You've got a friend!

All About Dogs

Whether you have a hero or a ham,
a genius or a lovable mutt,
learn a little about the dog in your life!

If a dog is your best friend, you have history on your side! Dogs are believed to be the oldest of domesticated animals. The bond between dogs and humans goes back at least 14,000 years, although some genetic discoveries suggest that the relationship may date back over 100,000 years to a time when people spent most of their days hunting the early friends and relatives of those DNA-crazed pets in Jurassic Park.

A dog's family tree goes back to the wolf line, where at some ancient points wolves became more doglike. The four dogs considered most ancient are the dingo, the New Guinea singing dog, the African basenji, and the greyhound. Where your neighbor's barking dog—the one who keeps you awake all night—comes from, no one knows.

A dog-size dog! In some breeds the size difference between a grown male and grown female can be as much as 6 inches in overall length and 40 pounds or more in weight. So if you love a large-size breed—mastiffs, Bernese mountain dogs, even boxers—but wish they weren't "that big," choosing a female might be the answer.

Living in a condo or small apartment and thinking of bringing home a four-legged friend? Consider teaming up with a small- to mid-size dog such as a schnauzer, sheltie, Lhasa apso, shih tzu, or cocker spaniel. Avoid breeds known for herding, hunting, barking, or digging such as retrievers or hounds. You both will be happier.

Poodles, Portuguese water dogs, and Kerry blue and Welsh terriers are "nonshedding" breeds. Their coats do shed, but not on the furniture. These dogs rely on regular grooming—from a person—to comb out dead hair and keep skin healthy.

The thickness and health of a dog's coat can be affected by stress, cold weather, diet, illness, pregnancy, and changes in hormone levels. Keeping in touch with your dog's coat and skin can give you an idea as to what's going on underneath it.

Take care of your longhair! Long, silky coats such as those of the Maltese, Afghan hound, and Yorkshire terrier should receive daily combing and brushing to keep them detangled. A slicker brush does the trick, as does a pin brush, which is less damaging to the coat.

Spaying or neutering is a health boost for dogs. Problems associated with the reproductive system are reduced or eliminated, and research shows that cancer rates are drastically reduced. Neutering also produces positive behavioral benefits and helps control pet overpopulation.

Those unsightly rings… If your dog has ring around his leather collar, try using a colorfast fabric or nylon one. If the collar gets wet, take it off the dog until both dog and collar are dry.

Whole lot of chewin' goin' on? Owners of aggressive chewers find that latex and solid rubber chew toys last longer than other kinds. Vinyl or rope toys are fine for the less determined. Any kind of toy is better than shoes, furniture, or houseplants!

The grass is always greener… or is it? No one really knows why dogs eat grass. False theories abound, but no dog has yet come forward with the truth. Maybe dogs just like the taste. An occasional munch won't hurt, but make sure the lawn has not been recently treated with chemical fertilizers or pesticides. That's a salad dressing no dog needs!

Does your dog rub his ears on the ground a lot, or groan and lean into your hands as you handle his head? This is a likely sign of an ear infection. Your veterinarian can prescribe effective treatment.

Floppy-eared breeds have a special charm of their own, but those flippity-floppy ears run a higher risk of infection. Normal air circulation is cut off allowing moisture to collect underneath the ear flap, an invitation to excess bacteria and yeast. If you notice your dog starting to show signs of infection, try tying the dog's ears up on top of his head for a few hours to help air things out. It looks pretty crazy, but think of it as a hip hair style!

Fido vs the Flea

It's a wrestling match repeated each year! In one corner, your dog. Everywhere else, a tag team army of fleas. How can the good guy win? Take the offensive! Success requires regular, correct use of flea control products, cleaning, grooming, and an early start. Put fleas down for the count!

🐾 Ninety-nine percent of the flea population exists as eggs, larvae, and pupae—no wonder fleas are so difficult to reason with! So, for an effective control program you need to target bedding, the yard, and your house, as well as the dog himself.

🐾 If you live in a year-round mild climate, flea infestation is a constant threat. Frigid winters at least kill off the fleas outdoors, but fleas can continue to prosper indoors. Regular vacuuming and housecleaning help with the battle.

❤ Pyrethrin, a chemical extract from dried chrysanthemums, is a gentle, effective product for puppies and sick or aging dogs. It is a safe flea control choice for your sensitive dog.

❤ Flea bite dermatitis, the result of a dog's allergy to flea saliva, can cause severe skin problems for your pooch. As the dog scratches and bites, the skin has no chance to heal. Special bath products, including soothing oatmeal baths you can buy from a groomer, can help.

❤ Regular and careful use of flea dips, shampoos, and other treatments, along with house and yard controls, go a long way in keeping your dog on the winning end of any flea fight. Sick 'em!

🐾 Suck 'em up! Vacuuming your carpets helps to remove any flea eggs hiding there, but be sure to throw out or burn the vacuum bag afterward, or the little monsters will hatch inside it. Be it a bag, brush, or body, fleas can call it home.

🐾 The best time to control the flea population is before it explodes in the spring. House and yard sprays that contain growth-inhibiting chemicals are most effective if in place before the first eggs are laid.

🐾 Flea combing can effectively pick up fleas from the main trouble spots on the dog: the top of the head, base of the ears, stomach, and ear flaps. Frequent flea combing is a good way to monitor the effectiveness of your efforts. Here's a tip: dip the comb in an insecticide before each pass to kill the fleas it traps.

❀ Regularly grooming your dog helps eradicate fleas. Daily brushing and combing keep the coat mat-free and prevent the buildup of flea hiding places. Weekly bathing sends the little buggers floating away.

❀ Some flea control products can be toxic if used incorrectly. Read labels carefully and follow instructions. Contact your vet if your pet exhibits any reactions to a product.

❀ Dog owners and veterinarians report excellent results in the flea-for-all against fleas when using some monthly flea control products. Some once-a-month oral medications, and monthly topical applications, are available from your veterinarian.

Today, dog breeds number approximately four hundred, of which two hundred or so are registered by breed clubs and societies. Some breeds are represented by only a few registered individuals, while other breeds such as German shepherds and cocker spaniels are represented by thousands.

A dog whose hair stands out wildly after a bath is usually not doing a Don King imitation. Static electricity is the culprit. If you don't want to leave things as they are, having fun scaring neighbors and friends, you can neutralize the charges by using humectant or emollient conditioners, sprays, or rinses made for dogs. Keeping the house humidity level at 50 percent also helps.

Dogs with short, pushed-in faces have more trouble breathing in hot, humid weather. Curtail strenuous exercise during hot spells.

Black and other dark-colored dogs suffer more from excessive heat than their lighter-colored cousins. Make sure there is plenty of water and extra shade for dark-colored dogs during the summer.

No matter what breed your dog, keep his ears clean and dry. Bacteria and yeast are always present in a dog's ears, but a change in temperature, air flow, or humidity can cause the bacteria to multiply resulting in an ear infection. Keep ears clean to prevent problems.

Tick Trick: To remove ticks from your dog, kill the pests by directly applying alcohol or fingernail polish remover onto them. Wait a few minutes, then remove the tick with tweezers. Don't crush the little varmints between your fingers—they carry diseases that can affect humans. Avoid direct contact by wearing gloves—as long as they are not baseball or boxing gloves.

To remove a tick when no tweezers can be found, use your index finger to apply gentle circular pressure on the skin surrounding the tick until it drops off. Remember: Don't touch or squash a tick with your bare hands.

To determine if your dog is overweight, place your thumbs on the dog's backbone and run your fingers along the rib cage. You should be able to feel the bony part of each rib easily. If not, it's time to shed some poundage. Another tip-off is if the dog is starting to look like a bowling ball.

Long walks on short legs... Pop-top water bottles make it easy to give your walking companion a drink along the way. Put the pop-top in your dog's cheek and squeeze the bottle carefully.

Care 'n' Comfort

Taking care of your
four-legged friend
from nose to toes

How about a new way to spoil your pet? Consider a dog-size water bed! Actually, water beds soothe sore muscles and bones, and can be a real help to an arthritic or senior dog.

Doggy day care is a new option for urban, working pet owners who agonize over leaving a pet home alone to face boredom and solitude. These centers can provide stimulating environments and supervised play groups. Select a provider as carefully as you would one for your children.

Is Lassie constantly barking? Make time each day to engage your dog in playful activities or in obedience training. The dog wants attention and some mental stimulation. Most likely, she's bored!

It All Depends on the Weather!

Whether it's hot and humid or wintry and windy, the state of the weather calls for some common sense. Make sure your dog weathers the weather!

🐾 Realize that puppies and house dogs are not acclimated to being outside. If it's too cold or hot outside for you, it's that way for Fido, too. Any dog who spends time outdoors in winter needs adequate shelter and water that's not frozen. Any dog spending time outdoors in summer heat needs protective shade and plenty of water in a bowl that can't be tipped over.

🐾 Did you know that dogs can sunburn? Those with light-colored skin on their nose and ears are prime candidates for sunburn and skin cancer if they spend countless hours outside in the hot sun. Think about what you would do as a preventative—apply sunscreen to exposed areas! Hairless breeds should wear sunblock during the day. Fine-coated breeds benefit from wearing a "wet coat" of chamois cloth soaked in water.

❀ Canine Caution! Heatstroke can be life threatening. If your dog is panting excessively and has purple or gray gums, cool her down immediately with wet towels, ice, and water at the base of the neck. Veterinary treatment may be required.

❀ In summertime, it should go without saying that you don't leave your dog in a parked car with the windows rolled up! Yet, people do just that for a "quick run" into a store or the post office. Unfortunately, the temperature inside a car can climb quickly to more than 100 degrees Fahrenheit. Your dog could suffer heatstroke, or even death. Leave the dog home.

❀ Take note of the temperature. On a hot, humid day, a dog can get heatstroke even while playing in the water! Don't overdo playtime on hot days. Because dogs depend on panting to cool themselves, there is a limit to how much heat they can blow off. Think smart!

🐾 Summer fun? Be aware that pool decks, truck beds, and asphalt can heat up and burn the pads of a dog's feet. Avoid leaving your dog on such surfaces for any length of time, or outfit your dog with a set of nylon or leather booties.

🐾 In winter, frostbite and hypothermia are the two most dangerous conditions facing your dog. In subzero temperatures, a dog's pads and ears are susceptible to freezing. Frigid temperatures can also freeze a dog's water supply quickly; and eating snow doesn't provide sufficient liquid to prevent hypothermia problems. Cold is never comfortable. If your dog is ill or in a weakened condition, keep her indoors during any cold weather.

🐾 Evaluate your dog's diet depending on the season. A dog who is extra-active in the spring may need increased calories, as would a dog spending cold winter nights outside. For the summer doldrums, consider smaller portions or reduced-calorie food. But avoid vigorous exercise with your dog in any type of extreme weather.

Good grief! It's grooming time! Keeping your dog clean and groomed not only improves appearance but also keeps Fido fit and healthy. Just by regular brushing, you increase circulation, distribute oils, and remove dirt and dead skin.

Bathing—the best way to prevent skin problems—maintains a healthy coat. After bathing, rinse your dog's coat thoroughly. Shampoo residue can irritate a dog's sensitive skin.

Canine Caution! When using "natural" shampoo products, be careful of those containing citrus. Citrus products can cause irritation to sensitive skin and eyes. Also, "All Natural" doesn't necessarily mean nontoxic.

Keep your dog happy, healthy, and polite with plenty of interaction, walks, and playtime. An exercised dog is less hyper and easier to manage than a couch potato.

Don't become a house slug! Simple walking invigorates you physically and energizes you emotionally. You can exercise, train your dog, and watch her play all at the same time. And, it's free!

chapter 2

When brushing your dog's coat, brush the hair, not the skin! Brushing too roughly can cause "brush burn" and make the dog unwilling to be groomed in the future.

Blow-drying and brushing your dog at the same time helps loosen a shedding coat. Use a low setting to avoid burning the dog's skin. A special grooming dryer makes the job easier.

Cutting your dog's hair short won't eliminate shedding. A short coat may be easier to manage, but the dog will still shed. Pretty sneaky!

For your white or light-colored dog, select a shampoo that claims to brighten light-colored coats. For black dogs, there are specially formulated shampoos that bring out the sheen in a dark coat. Leave these shampoos on for several minutes before rinsing. There are also tearless shampoos for the head and face.

Hair all over the brush? Cut a section from an old nylon stocking and slip it over the head of the brush before grooming. Make sure the bristles poke through. To remove the hair, simply pull up the nylon.

Poodles, Old English sheepdogs, and other breeds with a lot of hair in their ears, should have that hair removed. Excess hair in the ear canal can lead to infections. A vet can take care of this for you.

Earwax buildup leads to chronic moisture in the ear and decreases light and air flow into the ear canals. Some dogs produce more wax than others. Keep the ears clean. To dislodge old wax, use a cotton ball moistened with mineral oil.

When trimming nails, cut just before the quick to avoid pain and bleeding. If the nails are light, you can see the pinkish quick. If dark, cut where the nail begins to curl.

Trimming excess hair between your dog's toes can eliminate places for ticks to hide as well as reduce the possibility of anything becoming embedded between the toes. Be especially careful of that area, however. It is easy to cut the dog, and a ticklish dog could move her paw just as you're snipping.

Regular bathing, brushing, ear cleaning, and toenail trimming are important no matter what breed your dog. Shorthaired, sleek-coated dogs don't have much hair, but they still need to be groomed. End your sessions with a doggy treat. Hugs and kisses are always nice, too!

chapter 2

When bathing your dog, mix equal amounts of shampoo and water in a spray bottle and spray the dog. This method applies shampoo evenly and avoids waste!

Canine Caution! Make sure nail trimmers are sharp. Dull trimmers can tear the nail. To assure a clean cut, clip each nail deliberately, squeezing the trimmers together quickly.

To remove gum from your dog's coat, freeze the spot with an ice cube, then apply peanut butter and wipe off. Freezing makes the gum manageable, and peanut oil loosens it.

Brushing your dog's teeth at least twice a week with a doggy toothpaste and a soft toothbrush helps prevent dental problems. Cavities in dogs are uncommon, but more than 85 percent of dogs suffer from periodontal disease. To get Smiley accustomed to the ritual, rub the teeth and gums with cheesecloth dipped in bullion. Gradually replace the bullion with toothpaste.

Canine Caution! Never use human toothpaste to clean your dog's teeth. Dogs are elegant and don't spit, so they must swallow the toothpaste, and that can mean an upset stomach. Use a specially formulated dog toothpaste for canine choppers.

Lost dog? If you act quickly and offer a reward, you have a 90 percent chance of finding your missing pooch. Dogs with current identification tags are the ones most likely to be returned. For more peace of mind, consider tattooing or having a microchip placed painlessly under your dog's skin.

A little lower to the left... Any form of massage that is good for people is likely to benefit your dog as well. Knead the muscles of the neck, working your fingers in small circles behind each ear, and travel down the back of the neck, then along each side of the spine. Massage can improve your dog's health, behavior, and quality of life. The trick is teaching the dog to massage you!

Take new routes when you go for walks or runs. A variety of locations helps maintain your dog's mental health—and yours!

Does your dog seem lonesome or listless? Consider bringing home a canine companion to keep your dog company when you are not around. Dogs are pack animals and generally are social. A temporary or permanent pal can be a pick-me-up!

To remove tar from your dog's coat, liberally apply vegetable oil to the tar and leave on overnight. Bathe the dog the next day. The oil causes the tar to slide off the hair shaft.

Your Good Ol' Dog

Treat aging and senior dogs with special care. Here are some things to consider that can make the elder statesman of the house chipper and comfortable.

🐾 Senior dogs often lack the body fat they need to tolerate winter cold. If you don't want to be out in the weather, neither does your dog—and the dog doesn't get bundled up!

🐾 Some Crank Advice: A dog's tail contains a large blood supply. So, "cranking" your old dog's tail—as though starting up a Model T—actually can relieve spinal compression and assist in circulation!

❧ If you notice that your dog has lost flexibility and limberness, is not as playful as usual, and is reluctant to continue on long walks, arthritis may be the cause. Cold, damp weather makes things worse. Your veterinarian can alleviate the problem with a combination of medication and diet changes or, in advanced cases, surgery.

❧ Keep a close eye out for lumps, bumps, or other changes in your older dog's body. Grooming sessions are helpful for spotting changes that might signal health problems. Run a head-to-toe check regularly.

❧ Older dogs should undergo regular checkups for such age-related problems as cancer, arthritis, heart disease, and bad gums and teeth. Proper diet and exercise go a long way toward keeping older dogs feeling and acting young!

❀ Older dogs can be kept fit and healthy with regular exercise and activity. If your veteran dog is showing signs of arthritis, swimming sessions in warm, shallow water under close supervision can be helpful.

❀ Kidney disease is the leading cause of death in older dogs. You can decrease strain on your dog's kidneys by lowering her food's protein levels as she ages. As protein quantity decreases, quality becomes more important. Good food, good health!

Indoors, Outdoors, All Around the House

Be it ever so humble,
give Fido a home!

House dogs are prone to boredom. They need daily interaction and stimulation to ward off disruptive behavior. Choose play toys and chews that provide active entertainment such as weighted balls that roll in unpredictable directions and rubber chews in differing shapes and textures. It's not Las Vegas, but it beats the same old routine.

Dogs make lousy students of electrical engineering. If your pet loves to chew, he may well decide to chew a tasty lamp cord or TV plug—a shocking proposition. Keep electrical cords out of the way and try dusting them with cayenne pepper to deter your favorite chewer.

If your too-smart dog has figured out a way to escape from your fenced yard, consider building an enclosed dog run. Your dog will be able to enjoy the outdoors without the dangers beyond the fence.

When walking your dog, hold firmly to the leash so a sudden rush doesn't result in the dog breaking free and heading into trouble or traffic. Consider a double-handled leash if the dog becomes more than you can handle.

Keep your dog a paw's length from postal workers, meter readers, and door-to-door solicitors who might call when you're not home. It is best for all involved if your trusty watchdog doesn't have a clear shot at them!

Nondomesticated animals are likely to carry diseases that are harmful to your pet. Don't allow your dog any physical contact with these wild critters. An occasional card or letter will have to suffice.

If the fragrance from the dog run is less than lovely, you can eliminate those outdoor odors by diluting 1 cup of laundry bleach in 2 gallons of water. Use a watering can to apply wherever needed.

All Around the Doghouse

Dogs are den animals and enjoy having a place of their own. Provide your pal with a special area to call home. Here are some home improvement tips designed to make your dog the king or queen of the castle!

🐾 For style, bigger isn't always better. Choose a doghouse that enables your dog to stand up, turn around, and lie down comfortably inside. Remember: The less square footage the doghouse has, the better it will retain heat to keep your dog warmer on cold evenings and in winter.

🐾 Avoid any doghouse that has protruding nails or rough or sharp edges. These can cause injury.

❧ Use nontoxic paint when painting a doghouse. Many dogs choose to chew on their surroundings.

❧ Like your own house, your dog's house needs a slanted roof so rain or snow won't accumulate and weigh it down. Also, a removable roof style makes for easy cleaning.

❧ A baffle or canvas flap over the doorway helps keep wind and rain outside your puppy's palace. Clear plastic flaps allow your dog to see out and you to see in.

❅ Line the doghouse with a pad, blanket, or straw for comfort. Cedar shavings help repel fleas. Clean the bedding regularly to remove odors and kill fleas.

❅ During flea season, treat the doghouse bedding and interior with a pyrethrin-based spray or powder each week. A clean house makes for a happy dog!

❅ After providing a shelter for your dog, don't end up in the doghouse for neglect! Wipe down mats, wash any blankets, and eliminate fleas, which could end up in your home. A clean doghouse will be used more often and can help you avoid extra housecleaning.

Canine Caution! Working on the family car? Be careful with the fluids. Sweet-smelling antifreeze and radiator coolant attract curious dogs. Just a few drops ingested are enough to kill a puppy or small dog. Clean up any spills immediately and thoroughly. Better yet, use nontoxic antifreeze, which is available at most auto supply stores.

Unchain My Heart: A dog chained outdoors is vulnerable to wild animals, other dogs, and dognappers. Chaining restricts the dog's mobility and defenses. If you absolutely must restrict the dog's mobility outdoors, fences or kennels are safer alternatives.

Canine Caution! Keep kitchen and bathroom cupboard doors closed. Cleaning supplies, chemicals, and even their containers can pose a serious health threat to curious dogs. Consider installing latches if your dog has a magic touch with doors.

Totally trashed! Chicken bones, cellophane wrappers, chocolate, and broken glass are only a few of the potentially lethal treasures your garbage-can raider can come across in the household trash. Be safe. Keep cans secured and out of harm's (the dog's) way.

Fertilizers, cleaning supplies, and pesticides are potentially lethal if your dog decides to give them a taste. Never store chemicals in open containers around the yard or garage. Store them in leak-proof receptacles to keep curious sniffers safe.

Canine Caution! Many garden plants and houseplants are poisonous to dogs. Curious puppies run the greatest risk of eating toxic greenery. Oleander, holly, dieffenbachia, philodendron, daffodil bulbs, and morning glories are a few common offenders. Tomato and potato vines are toxic if eaten. Your vegetable and flower gardens should be off-limits to four-legged landscapers.

If your dog is confined indoors, make sure he has access to a window or patio door so he can at least see outside. Where possible, install a dog door to give Rover access to an enclosed outdoor run or yard.

If your lawn shows yellow spots from your dog urinating on it, have your vet examine the dog to see if he can be switched to a food with less protein. Excess protein can lead to a uric acid imbalance that causes those yellow spots.

Oh where, oh where has my little dog gone? An increasingly popular method of doggy identification is the microchip surgically implanted under a dog's skin. Many animal shelters routinely scan new arrivals in hopes of identifying them. Your vet can turn Fido into high-tech Fideaux!

Dog tags are a big help with getting your lost dog back home. If you're on-line, add your e-mail address to the ID tags. Also, if your dog has a medical condition, list that information on the tag.

Chow Time!

No more suspicion
about doggy nutrition

What is the most common, nutrition-related health condition in dogs? Obesity. Experts estimate that 25 to 30 percent of adult dogs in the United States are greatly overweight or on the road to becoming so. If your dog needs to lose weight, ask your veterinarian about reduced-calorie food. Don't let your puppy turn into a piggy.

To make sure your dog food matches your dog's needs, read the product purpose statement on pet food labels. If you have a growing dog, for example, pick a product specially formulated for growth.

Fad diets for people seldom work, and the same is true for dogs. If your dog is overweight, ask your vet about getting your dog on a diet. Don't be swept into the latest canine diet fad.

When the label shouts, "Bowser Meal for Titanic Dogs!" you'll want to read the ingredients list on the dog food label to find out what you are actually feeding your dog. Ingredients must be listed in descending order of concentration. If poultry is listed first, then poultry is the primary ingredient. If pulverized pig toes is listed first, well…

Primary Ingredient: Pulverized Pig toes

In selecting a dog food, some owners prefer a product that is "naturally preserved." It is important to remember, however, that some natural preservatives have a much shorter shelf life than traditional chemical preservatives. Pay attention to freshness.

The AAFCO (Association of American Feed Control Officials) is a nongovernmental agency that sets standards for the nutrition in your dog's food. If a dog food label carries the statement "Animal feeding tests using AAFCO procedures substantiate that (Name of Product) provides complete and balanced nutrition..." you know that the food was actually fed to dogs and found to be adequate. A statement that reads "(Name of Product) is formulated to meet the nutritional levels established by the AAFCO..." means the food was not actually fed to dogs but was analyzed and compared to recognized standards.

Doing a load of household dishes? Wash the dog's dishes, too. Bacteria builds up quickly in food and water dishes.

Under the "Guaranteed Analysis" section of a dog food label, you will find the basic formula of the food expressed as a percentage of protein, fat, fiber, and water. Other than water or "moisture," protein should rank highest.

Feeding dogs a low-protein diet can make sense if you're treating medical or postsurgical bladder stones. Adding salt to the diet increases water intake, further decreasing the likelihood of crystal or stone formation.

Dogs can occasionally be allergic to an ingredient such as corn or soybeans in their foods. Allergy tests done by a veterinarian can pinpoint a problem. A food change can make a big difference to a "sick" dog.

Stop the shivers! In extreme cold, dogs expend a lot of energy just to stay warm; thus, they need extra calories to generate body heat. During winter months, serve your fearless ice hound plenty of food with higher fat and protein contents.

Let's NOT have some cookies and milk with Fido! Certain common foods can be dangerous to dogs. Chocolate, even in small amounts, can be toxic; cow's milk cannot be properly digested by puppies. Resist the temptation to share your snack food with your dog— unless you've opted for dog biscuits and puppy treats!

Chow Time!

Check expiration and packaging dates on dog food just as you would the "use by" dates for human food. Avoid packages that appear to have been wet, torn, or crushed at some point.

A dog who suddenly rejects foods she has previously eaten enthusiastically might be signaling that the food is stale or spoiled. Keep food fresh, and don't let it sit outdoors in a dog dish, especially in summer.

Is Lassie becoming finicky over food? Dogs usually respond well to any food given them by hand. This also works for medications and pills that the dog refuses. Hide the pill in a piece of food and offer it by hand.

If your dog likes to graze on grass regularly, consider adding small amounts of steamed vegetables to her diet. Your dog may actually like greens, need the greens for roughage and digestion, or may just be trying to expand her culinary horizons.

chow Time!

Even dry dog food can go bad if stored improperly. After opening, kibbles should be kept in a dry, cool environment. Your dog's eating habit is your key to food purchases. Buy enough so that you're not running to the store every other day, but not so much that a bag will sit for a month.

Weak bones, dull coat, and lack of energy: If this applies to your significant other, consider a replacement. If it applies to your dog, a protein deficiency could be the culprit.

Canine Caution! Chocolate candy is dandy but not for dogs. The theobromine—a stimulant related to caffeine—in chocolate can cause a dangerous reaction. Don't fall into the trap of thinking, "just one little piece" is fine. Be safe and choose a treat specifically made for dogs.

Happiness Is a Warm...

The special world
of puppies

If you're bringing your new puppy home from a breeder or a shelter, try to get something that the puppy is used to such as a blanket or toy. A new home is less frightening if familiar scents are nearby.

When a new puppy arrives on the scene, a longtime family dog can feel neglected. Prevent sibling rivalry and feelings of neglect by spending extra time with your first dog. Reinforce the good relationship you have with Fido I.

Feed, groom, and bed down your puppy in the same locations each time. This helps the pup associate a specific place with a specific activity and teaches him what is expected. Be careful of what you teach. If you allow a puppy to sleep with you at night, guess where the grown dog will want to sleep!

Canine Caution! Be careful when using a heating pad to warm a new litter of puppies. Too much heat can cause painful burns on newborns. Warm is wonderful; hot is not!

A puppy's canine teeth should fall out after two or three months. If they don't, it's best to have them removed by a veterinarian to avoid overcrowding brought on by the permanent teeth poking through before the "baby teeth" have been shed.

Don't try to turn your young pup into an Arnold Schwarzenegger. Too much strenuous activity before the pup truly matures can inhibit bone development. Wait until at least eight months of age before "pumping up" your pup or starting any kind of serious conditioning program.

They owe it all to Mom! A pup needs to be with his mother and littermates for at least eight to ten weeks to learn how to be a dog. After that, it's up to the owner to fill in as teacher.

Puppies like to sleep in a small, confined place and feel safe retreating to a special place when tired or overwhelmed. A crate can make a nifty nap spot for your puppy. Children should be taught that it's puppy quiet time when their pal is in the crate. Like small children, puppies need naps and plenty of rest!

Chapter 5

Teething Tip: A piece of towel knotted, dampened, and chilled a bit in the fridge comfortably massages tender gums as the puppy chews it. Make sure this teething toy is large enough for the puppy to carry and chew on without swallowing.

Avoid hard, crunchy biscuits and chewy, hard-to-swallow treats for training your puppy. Tasty, easily managed morsels keep your puppy's attention focused on you rather than on battling the food.

In puppies, heart problems caused by birth defects may be correctable with surgery. Early diagnosis is vital. If left uncorrected, permanent damage could result.

Playin' Around: Puppies need play to develop their full physical potential. Playing builds and strengthens bone and muscle. This interactive exercise is good for both of you!

The most dangerous time in a pup's life is when his natural maternal antibody levels are still high enough to interfere with vaccines, yet too low to protect against disease. These antibodies decline somewhere between the ages of six to sixteen weeks. To fully cover your pup during this period, vaccinations are recommended at six to eight, twelve to fourteen, and sixteen to eighteen weeks of age.

Although your pup (probably) won't have to face that first spring dance, interaction and exposure to other dogs and people is important for his social makeup. Poorly socialized dogs rarely develop appropriate behavior and can tempt an owner to do the unthinkable—send the dog to a shelter. Keep everybody happy: introduce your dog to the world!

The best way to prevent your dog from biting is to begin socializing him from puppyhood. As part of a structured training program, exposing him to a variety of situations and places works wonders.

A Puppy Nip Tip: If your playful pup has taken to nipping your hands during playtime, pour Listerine mouthwash over your hands before beginning. One or two nips will likely convince the little rascal there are tastier things to bite!

Cradle rather than carry! Teach small children to cradle puppies in their laps rather than pick pups up and carry them. Squirming pups are easy to drop, and their developing joints are easily dislocated or sprained.

Puppies experience periods of rapid bone growth. During this time, a balanced growth diet and adequate—not strenuous— daily exercise play important roles in minimizing the onset of hip dysplasia.

Handling your puppy's feet on a regular basis makes nail trimming or attending to the paw much easier later on. Hold the paws one at a time, gently but firmly, and give praise or a treat afterward.

Growing puppies need a dry kibble that is between 26 to 32 percent protein. Dry foods made specifically for large-breed puppies contain less protein to slow the rate of rapid growth so there is less stress on growing bones and joints. In any event, your puppy is becoming a mature dog quick as a tail wag!

Rabies vaccine can be given as early as twelve to sixteen weeks, if necessary. Getting the rabies vaccination at the same time as the last parvovirus vaccine helps avoid maternal antibody interference.

Puppies and Primping

Don't be afraid to start grooming your pup at an early age. Conditioning a young dog to the sound and feel of clippers will make the job much easier when it's time to use them on the grown-up version.

🐾 You can bathe a puppy as young as eight weeks old, but see it from the puppy's point of view—"What the heck is going on?!" Water and washing can be frightening to an uninitiated pup, so never spray water directly into the face and don't place the pup under running water. A hard stream of water can feel like Niagara Falls to a young dog. Keep water out of the ears by placing cotton balls just inside the openings.

🐾 A puppy's nails are small and may be difficult to trim. Try using small scissors or human nail trimmers at first. After the puppy gets a little older, the nails harden and you can switch to regular canine nail trimmers. Consider using a professional groomer for the first trims. Groomers are experienced with twisting, squirming pups.

🐾 Keep grooming sessions short and sweet, even if it means saving the nail clipping or full brush-out until the next day. Puppies are like small children— their attention span can shift rapidly! Make grooming a positive experience for both of you. Praise the pup when he sits still, and reward him with a special treat after your session. Your attitude makes a big difference in how a puppy views bathing and grooming!

Happiness Is a Warm...

Mirror, mirror on the wall… Puppies are not as vain as people, but most puppies get a kick out of mirrors. You can decrease boredom for your little star by mounting mirrors in a play area. This helps with the pup's socialization and usually provides your tyke with amusement.

What is your pup learning? It may not be the ABC's or advanced computer technology, but what he learns can spell the difference between a well-behaved dog and an unholy terror. Start early so you get the chance to control what the pup learns. You can't always teach an old dog new tricks, but you can teach a young dog new behavior!

Happy, Healthy Hounds

Vets, vaccinations,
and keeping Fluffy fit
and hearty at home

The normal, healthy heart rate for large dogs is 70 beats per minute. Smaller dogs may average 130. The human heart rate when seeing an irresistible puppy is incalculable!

Canine medicine and surgery technology is constantly advancing, leading to quality lives for dogs who in the past have had to struggle. A dog with an irregular heartbeat, for example, can have a pacemaker implanted by a board-certified specialist to keep the ol' ticker ticking away!

Dogs who are simply family pets generally do not need vaccinations against kennel cough, but dogs with increased exposure to other dogs at dog shows or those being left at kennels benefit from the vaccinations.

chapter 6

Canine Caution! Did you know that dogs can suffer the effects of secondhand smoke? A smoker's dog has a 50 percent greater chance of developing lung cancer than a nonsmoker's dog. Shorthaired breeds run the highest risk. Keep Smokey smokeless!

It is simply not true that spaying or neutering makes a dog fat and lazy. Dogs get fat and lazy for the same reasons people do: overeating and lack of exercise. "Fixing" your pet affects only reproduction and associated behaviors. Unless you're a serious breeder, have your dog spayed or neutered.

From acupuncture and acupressure to paw massage! Bolster your dog's immune system by rubbing the point located below the dewclaw. Rubbing the elbow from inside to outside helps general immune problems, including skin disorders.

Health insurance, yes or no? If you opt for it, make sure the company is licensed by the state. Find out who the underwriter is, and call your state's insurance commission to evaluate the company's stability and payout record.

From your nose to your dog's ear... Ear problems are often signaled by a strong odor, while healthy ears have little or no odor. If your nose gets an earful, schedule a visit to the vet.

Ears another signal. If your dog whimpers when you touch her ears, she could have an ear infection. For ears that are extrasensitive or extremely warm to the touch, call for a checkup.

A dog's ears can become infected for many reasons: parasites (ear mites are the most common), bacterial infections, or foreign objects that become lodged in the ear canal. A correct diagnosis is important. If your dog has ear mites, all the animals in the household should be treated. Look for signals such as head shaking and work with your vet.

Some Words on Lyme Disease

Lyme disease is the most common tick-transmitted illness in dogs. The disease is transmitted when an infected tick bites a dog and injects bacteria into the bloodstream. The bacteria move into joints and cause arthritic-type pain or lameness. They can also cause red spots on the skin for a period of weeks and can manifest themselves as a fever. As possible signs of infection, watch for tender, slightly swollen joints and early tiring.

🐾 Recent research shows that 70 percent of tick bites occur in residential backyards, not in the forests and bush as you would expect, so city living does not provide immunity! Check with your vet to see if the disease is prevalent in your area. Forty-seven of the forty-eight continental United States report Lyme disease.

🐾 Lyme disease can be confused with other conditions that affect the legs, heart, kidneys, and nervous system, so check with your veterinarian if you have any concerns. Treatment with antibiotics is needed. The best strategy is to vaccinate adult dogs if you have not already done so and to have puppies immunized as part of their vaccination series.

Heartworms are transmitted by infected mosquitoes. In addition to regular oral preventives, consider spraying a canine-safe bug repellent on your dog's coat during mosquito season.

Weakness, coughing, and intolerance to exercise are signs of heartworm infection. If the dog has adult heartworms, she must undergo closely supervised therapy before starting regular preventive medication.

Schedule an annual heartworm exam. Heartworms and other serious threats to your dog's health are easier and less expensive to prevent than to cure. A routine exam and blood test can keep any problems from getting out of hand.

Itching, skin biting, sneezing, watery eyes? If your dog exhibits these allergic reactions, consider allergy testing to discover the substances that trigger these reactions. Sometimes a food substance is the culprit, and a change in diet can offer relief.

If your dog is vomiting, has developed a rash, has dilated pupils, or cannot stand, suspect poisoning. Even without knowing the cause, general fluid therapy and antibiotics can increase your dog's chance for survival. Call the vet immediately.

If your dog is drinking abnormally large amounts of water, it could indicate the onset of diabetes. The disease can be diagnosed with a simple blood test by a vet and controlled with insulin shots at home.

By keeping your dog's teeth clean, you can limit or prevent such problems as bad breath, periodontal disease, and even heart disease. Brushing your dog's teeth and dental checkups keep those canine choppers chomping!

Night coughs? If your dog coughs a lot at night and wakes up hacking, she may be developing congestive heart disease. This can be controlled with medication, so seek a vet's advice.

If you notice hair that is shedding in patches accompanied by chewing and scratching, you may be watching a hair replacement commercial. However, if it relates to the dog, it can indicate a health problem. Stress, illness, allergies, or inadequate diet can cause excessive shedding. Time to visit the vet.

Demodectic mange causes thinning of the hair and bald spots. It is treatable, but once exhibited it can recur. Going into heat, traveling, or any form of stress can trigger a relapse. Dogs—and their owners—benefit with less stress in their lives.

Canine Caution! If your dog swallows something poisonous and you can't reach your veterinarian, call the National Animal Poison Control Center at (800) 548-2423. Help is available and could save your pet's life.

If your dog has a pulled muscle or has bad hips or elbows, gently massaging the injured spot can help. This increases blood flow in the area and promotes healing.

Protect your little sniffer from foxtails. The barbed grass can easily become embedded in a sniffing dog's nasal passages or between the nails in a paw, where it punctures the skin and causes serious infection. Be conscious of where your dog is playing or walking. If the dog begins sneezing violently in foxtail country, get to the vet immediately.

Canine Caution! Don't share your medicines. Medications that humans routinely use can cause injury or death to dogs. Animals can get an adverse reaction to even such common medications as ibuprofen. Give your dog only what is prescribed by your vet.

A dog who "scoots" across the ground on her hind end may need her anal sac emptied. Ask your vet to show you how to perform this simple procedure at home.

Pay close attention to your dog's mouth and teeth. Untreated gingivitis weakens the bones, gums, and other tissues supporting teeth. Bacteria from untreated periodontal problems can be absorbed through the bloodstream and infect internal organs, including the heart.

The Great Outdoors

The great outdoors isn't so great if your dog encounters any of Mother Nature's little stingers and biters. Here are some emergency first aid measures:

🐾 For bee and wasp stings, remove the stinger with tweezers and apply cold compresses. If the dog shows signs of an allergic reaction such as swelling or rapid to difficult breathing get to the vet. Shock can occur within thirty minutes.

🐾 For black widow bites, apply cold compresses and get veterinary treatment immediately. Black widow venom is more poisonous than rattlesnake venom.

🐾 Snakes can be found in each of the forty-eight continental United States, in places far removed from hiking trails. With speedy care, however, 75 percent of snakebite cases survive. The key is getting to the vet quickly. If your dog gets bitten by a snake, carry her or use a makeshift transport for her rather

than let her walk any distance. Exercise spreads the venom faster.

✿ Do not use ice or tourniquets for snakebites. Venom greatly constricts the blood vessels, and ice constricts them further. Tourniquets do not completely prevent absorption of the venom, and they halt beneficial blood flow to the area.

✿ If the dog goes into shock from a poisonous bite, you can perform CPR: Push on the dog's chest to compress her heart and force blood to the brain. Then, hold the mouth closed and breathe into the nose. Repeat.

✿ Snakebites in the facial area that would not otherwise be fatal can kill a dog because airways become constricted through swelling. Keep the dog quiet and calm. The sooner antivenin can be administered, the better your dog's chance for survival.

The "Creeping Chubbies" is one of the biggest problems facing domestic dogs. If Fifi is adding pounds, the risks of hypertension and congestive heart failure increase. Keep the chubbies from advancing. Feed your dog a balanced diet and provide plenty of exercise.

A dog who exhibits obsessive-compulsive behavior such as constantly biting or sucking herself may have a form of epilepsy. To alleviate the symptoms, your vet can prescribe antiseizure medications.

If your dog must undergo major surgery, ask for a preanesthetic profile from the vet. This identifies any unknown problems that could surface with the anesthetic. Dogs with undiagnosed heart, liver, or blood conditions require special precautions.

chapter 6

Most dogs afflicted with heart disease show definite symptoms, including labored breathing, coughing, weakness, and fainting. Modern drugs and surgery can reduce or correct many problems, but early diagnosis is essential. Schedule a checkup with your vet if you notice possible symptoms.

Let your fingers do some walking! Moderate massage can help a dog recover from surgery and illness more quickly. It can also relieve pain from strained muscles and hip dysplasia and improve circulatory disorders.

An elixir for licks! Toy breeds are prone to excessive licking. Try spraying Bitter Apple or lemon water on your hands and chin. You won't be as tasty, so it should slow down that overactive tongue.

The Top Dog Syndrome: According to a dog's social hierarchy, the biggest, strongest, most dominant dog gets the best food first. Make sure you feed yourself first at mealtimes so your pet recognizes you as "top dog." Maintain your dominant position, and your dog will be more obedient to you.

Lead, Don't Follow: By walking through doors first, and making the dog wait until you give permission to follow, you will avoid the mad dash and potential foot stumbling from an overly aggressive dog. A little training reaps big behavioral benefits!

Even if your dog has a natural territorial aggression, that shouldn't mean your guests have to fight a war just to see you. Obedience training is a must to maintain control of the aggression. Call in a professional trainer if this territoriality goes overboard with such actions as snapping at guests, attacking anything that moves, or building moats and bunkers around the yard.

Walking the dog shouldn't be treated as an exercise chore. How would you like to be cooped up in the same place day after day, and then hustled through a fresh environment (the neighborhood) without getting a chance to enjoy all that new stuff? Slow down and sniff the neighborhood!

If your dog exhibits aggression—such as growling or snapping—as you approach him while eating, consult a professional trainer as soon as possible.

Who's the trainer around here? Your dog can be irresistible and ingenious in training you to feed him an improper diet loaded with table food, cookies, and people treats. Don't encourage the weight gain and digestive problems improper nutrition brings. Stick to high-quality commercial dog foods and treats.

Leaving the dog unattended for a while? Don't leave him harnessed. A harness is best used as an active walking collar. Other than that, you're inviting it to be chewed.

You've got the magic touch… and it's one of the best ways to strengthen the human/dog bond! Dogs enjoy being petted. One theory is that your touch mimics the nudging and nose contact a dog has with his mother. A little love goes a long way!

Problem dog? Maybe not! All too often, behavioral problems are inadvertently caused by owners. Make sure the dog's environment is suitable for his unique personality and temperament: Does he have enough space? Do you exercise and interact together? Is he free from pain and in good health? Problem behavior usually has a cause.

Taking the Plunge?

Some dogs might take to water but most need lessons in how to swim. Here's how:

🐾 Take the dog into water just deep enough for his feet not to touch bottom. Firmly support the dog under the chest. As the dog begins to envision himself as Mark Spitz, head him toward the water's edge and gradually let go. Play lifeguard for your dog by making sure his head stays above water.

🐾 You might want to consider fitting Fido with a life preserver while he's learning to swim. If your dog tires from all that paddling, the preserver will keep him afloat until you get to him.

A dog feeling bored and unattended is likely to turn to destructive behavior such as chewing, digging, and barking. Counter this with taking time out for play. Invent games and activities that allow the dog interaction with you.

Your dog prefers your company, but when you must leave Bowser alone, do as much as possible to keep him stimulated and promote solitary play. Rotate the toys you leave so each day there's something "new." For some sound and motion, leave a television or radio on while you're out. After all, TV has been going to the dogs for years.

chapter 7

Planning a training regimen for your dog? Begin with basic health care. Bowser should be free of parasites and up-to-date with all vaccinations. A general checkup from the vet ensures that the dog is in good shape internally.

An exercised dog is a healthy dog. Physical activity with your dog helps build and strengthen canine muscles, bones, and joints. Exercise keeps organs functioning at top levels and helps prevent boredom and restlessness. Keep Rover fit and happy!

You can undo a lot of good training by allowing bad behavior to surface during play. Any activity you would not normally allow—such as chewing on clothing or attacking your hands—should be discouraged in playtime, too.

A Hiking We Will Go ...

Hiking and camping with your dog is a special treat. New areas, fresh air, walks, and hikes are a great elixir for both of you. You can even condition your dog to carry a backpack by starting out with lightweight items! Here are some things to keep in mind to keep the outdoors enjoyable:

🐾 Before taking off for the day, spray the dog thoroughly with a commercial, dog-safe insect repellent to reduce the chance of attracting any hitchhiking ticks or fleas. This is especially important in areas where Lyme disease is prevalent.

🐾 Keep your dog on a leash in the wilderness. Even small rodents bite in defense, and many carry diseases, including rabies.

🐾 Pack a *first* aid kit containing medical tape, adhesive pads, gauze, a cold pack, antibiotic ointment, and tweezers. This can be of aid to both of you.

🐾 In wilderness areas or rough terrain, consider using nylon dog booties for your hiking pal's feet. They prevent cut or torn paw pads and protect the feet without compromising mobility—no matter how much the squirrels might laugh.

🐾 Add a temporary tag to your dog's collar that states where you are camping. Tying a bright bandanna around the dog's neck makes it easier to spot him if he gets lost in the woods. Best solution: Don't let your dog wander!

Dogs in the wild instinctively seek confining spaces when threatened. If your dog hides under the bed or in a closet during a thunderstorm, don't drag him out in an attempt to comfort him. Instead, put some clothing or towels with your familiar scent next to the dog for reassurance. Or, if you are a bit squeamish about storms, jump in the closet too.

Another Storm Strategy: Turn on music and pull the shades during a thunder and lightning storm. This could lessen the dog's reaction to the loud noises. In severe cases of fright, your veterinarian can prescribe a tranquilizer.

Special Considerations

Ideas for active, inactive,
bounding, boarded,
and travel-trekking dogs

Is your dog becoming a middle-aged couch potato? Try introducing an agility course or new game into her life. As with people, dogs' tastes in fun and games change as they mature.

Dogs who love to swim are more prone to ear infections than are landlubbers. If your dog does a great Esther Williams or Mark Spitz imitation, be sure to thoroughly dry the ears afterward. Commercial ear cleaners change the pH of the inner ear and act as drying agents.

Say "Cheesebone." When photographing your dog, get down to the dog's level and move in close. Speak gently to attract the dog's attention, and take a variety of shots to capture canine expressions—which may include laughter depending on how you look crawling down there!

Don't leave me! If your dog exhibits separation anxiety, spread a collection of treats, chews, and toys on the floor as you are getting ready to leave. This distracts the dog momentarily, and she'll learn not to dread your departure. Then, all you need to do is work on your own separation anxiety!

Spray-on coat conditioners applied to a freshly bathed and dried coat give the hair a high sheen and moisturize your dog's skin. Spray lightly; too much makes the coat oily and attracts dirt easily.

Boarding your dog? Most top-quality kennels require that a guest be vaccinated against diseases such as kennel cough and the corona virus. Lassie should be current on all vaccinations at least two weeks prior to her kennel vacation. Vaccinations done at drop-off time are insufficient for immediate protection.

Female dogs frequently "blow" their coats—shed excessively—following a heat cycle, pregnancy, or nursing. Daily grooming helps speed the process and keeps unwanted hair off carpets and upholstery.

Has your trusty hunter encountered the wrong end of a skunk?
A bath in tomato juice or apple cider vinegar can work to remove
the toughest, smelliest odor problems.

A Little Traveling Music ...

The truly cosmopolitan dog is a travelwise veteran who has marked trees and sniffed bushes worldwide! Here are some things to keep in mind if you are adding to your pet's frequent flier miles or sharing drive time:

🐾 If you're flying with your dog but using an airline instead of your own wings, check into the regulations regarding dogs on airplanes. The federal Aviation Administration (FAA) specifies that dogs must be at least eight weeks old to fly. Some airlines won't accept animals at all during hot or cold weather. Plan ahead.

🐾 Tranquilizers for flying? While you might think it's kind to administer a light tranquilizer to a dog being air shipped, be aware that the pill can make the dog susceptible to breathing problems. Cramped cargo holds can make matters worse. Discuss the idea with your vet.

🐾 Traveling abroad? Ask your veterinarian about international health certificates. Foreign travel is filled with restrictions and certifications. Also, avoid traveling in hot summer months, and bring plenty of purified water for your dog. Dogs are affected by changes in water quality just as you are.

🐾 Buckle up Buffy! When auto transporting your dog in a carrier, run the seat belt through the handle on top of the carrier or between the bars and secure it. This is insurance against a sudden stop or sharp turn that could send the carrier tumbling.

🐾 Car travel can be stressful for both you and your pet, even if the pet is not driving. On trips, make frequent stops so your dog can stretch her legs and attend to bathroom duties. Take along familiar toys, blankets, and chews to relieve boredom and make the new environment more friendly.

🐾 Remember that a clean dog makes for a happier traveler. Groom your dog before heading out on a trip together. Also, premoistened baby wipes (without fragrance or alcohol) are handy for cleaning dirty paws along the way.

Chapter 8

Careful! Don't drop those grooming shears! Not only do you risk injury to yourself and your dog but a good pair of scissors needs to be realigned by a professional sharpener. Hold onto the shears and make sure that they stay in top condition.

Swimming pools can be dangerous to dogs, even if they are good swimmers. Keep an eye on your swimming dog to make sure she can get out of the pool when she wants. When covering a pool for the night or during winter "downtime," be sure the pool tarp is secured around the edges. Every year, dogs drown from walking across a pool cover they thought was a solid surface.

Most dogs drink their water "straight," not "on the rocks," so keep your dog's outdoor water supply from freezing in winter. Water bowl heaters are available at a variety of stores.

Collar Calculations

❧ Choose a collar at least 3/8 inch wide for a toy dog, and 1/2 inch or wider for a large dog. Wide collars eliminate pressure between the rings of the esophagus.

❧ Slip collars must allow for enough room to slip over the largest part of the dog's head. Run a measuring tape around the head, ears, and under the jaws at the neck; then add two inches.

❧ A buckle collar should fit snugly enough so it does not slip over the dog's head but still allows room for two fingers under the collar.

Introducing another dog into the family? For that first meeting, use neutral territory—a place that belongs to neither dog. Your present boss-of-the-ranch may feel that her property is being threatened if a stranger plops down in the middle of it. Many dogs are protective of their pillows, toys, and favorite spots.

Canine Caution! Never leave children, particularly infants and toddlers, alone with dogs. It may be "child's play" to you, but to the dog child's play or teasing can be considered a threat and provoke an aggressive response.

Ticks are tacky between toes. If you are taking your dog into the woods, check her ears, neck, and head frequently for ticks. Other overlooked hiding places are the tail and in between the toes.

One hairy problem… Never bathe a matted coat; it only worsens the condition. If your dog's coat is badly matted, apply a detangler to the dry coat, let it set for a few minutes, then brush. Otherwise, it's a trip to the groomer for a trim.

The Christmas season brings some special considerations. Remember that mistletoe and holly are poisonous to dogs. Keep them out of sniffing range. Also, electric cords from Christmas trees and other decorations can be tempting to a chewer. Bundle the cords with twist ties and place them out of sight for a safe and happy holiday.

chapter 8

The Canine IQ Test

Much has been made lately about the relative intelligence of dogs not only to other animals but also to humans. Here is a simple test that measures your dog's IQ in dealing with everyday matters:

	You	The Dog?
1. Who gets up each morning, drives through nerve-wracking traffic, and goes to work?	☐	☐
2. Who gets her food prepared then served without having to cook or clean up?	☐	☐
3. Who has a full-time chauffeur?	☐	☐
4. Who do you think is smarter?	☐	☐

Good luck with your wise and wonderful dog!

For more fun facts and authoritative advice about dogs, including health-care advice, grooming tips, training advice, and insights into the special joys and overcoming the unique problems of dog ownership, go to your local pet shop, bookstore, or newsstand and pick up your copy of *Dog Fancy* magazine today.

BowTie™ Press is a division of Fancy Publications, which is the world's largest publisher of pet magazines. For further information on your favorite pets, look for *Dogs USA*, *Puppies USA*, *Cat Fancy*, *Cats USA*, *Kittens USA*, *Bird Talk*, *Horse Illustrated*, *Reptiles*, *Aquarium Fish*, *Rabbits*, *Ferrets USA*, and many more.